BÔ YIN RÂ
(J. A. SCHNEIDERFRANKEN)

THE BOOK ON
RESURRECTION

Translated from the German by
B.A.REICHENBACH

Sterling Paperbacks

STERLING PAPERBACKS
An imprint of
Sterling Publishers (P) Ltd.
A-59, Okhla Industrial Area, Phase-II,
New Delhi-110020.
Tel: 26387070, 26386209; Fax: 91-11-26383788
E-mail: mail@sterlingpublishers.com
www.sterlingpublishers.com

The book on RESURRECTION
English translation © 2009 by B. A. Reichenbach.
This book is translation from the German of *Aufersstehung* by Bô Yin Râ (J.A. Schneiderfranken), published in 1926.
The copyright to the German text is held by
Kober Verlag, AG, Bern, Switzerland.

First Indian Edition 2010
ISBN 978 81 207 5195 8

All rights are reserved.
No part of this publication may be reproduced, stored in a retrieval system or transmitted, in any form or by any means, mechanical, photocopying, recording or otherwise, without prior written permission of the original publisher.

Printed in India

Printed and Published by Sterling Publishers Pvt. Ltd.,
New Delhi-110 020.

THE BOOK ON RESURRECTION

Bô Yin Râ is the spiritual proper name of the author and artist Joseph Anton Schneiderfranken (1876-1943). He was born in Aschaffenburg, Germany, and died in Massagno/Lugano, Switzerland, where he had lived since 1925. His formal education as a painter began at the Staedel Art Institute in Frankfurt/Main, Germany, and then took him to Vienna, Munich, and Paris.

The literary legacy of Bô Yin Râ includes forty titles, published between 1919 and 1939, in Germany and Switzerland. Thirty-two of these works comprise a closely related cycle which the author gathered under the title of *Hortus Conclusis (The Enclosed Garden)*. In his books he addresses questions and concerns that, in the language of religion and philosophy, pertain to "final things" —the mysteries of mortal and eternal life, of God, the origin and goal of human existence—and gives advice on how one ought to live this present life to "lay up treasures" in the life to come.

What sets these books apart form other writings on these topics is their author's background and horizon. Thus, he does not give the reader the results of learned thinking, speculations, and beliefs, but lucid insights into the objective structure of reality, based upon direct, reliable experience. His books, therefore, as he explains, are not intended to create "beliefs," nor any new "religion," but should instead be used as maps that guide the reader safely through the labyrinth of this existence to the goal that every spiritually concerns human beings finally desires to attain.

*Available in Sterling Paperbacks
Books by*

BÔ YIN RÂ

The Book of DIALOGUES

The Path to GOD

The book on RESURRECTION

The Book on SOLACE

The Meaning of THIS LIFE

The Book on HAPPINESS

The Book on LIFE BEYOND

The Book on the LOVING GOD

The Book on RAJA-YOGA

The Book on HUMAN NATURE

The Book on LOVE

ACKNOWLEDGMENT

For her careful reading
and many sensitive comments
I am again grateful to
Alice Glawe

CONTENTS

Preface 9

1 Resurrection 13

2 The Knowledge Of Sages 23

3 Effects Of Law And Chance 31

4 Wasted Labors 41

5 Mardi Gras of the Occult 55

6 Inner Voices 67

7 The Magic Effect of Fear 81

8 The Limits Of Omnipotence 93

9 The New Life 107

10 Festive Joy 121

11 The Virtue of Laughter 133

12 Self-Conquest 141

   Conclusion 155

PREFACE

THERE SURELY IS NO NEED especially to justify the reason why I chose the heading given the first of the following twelve chapters also as the title that symbolically comprises the entire book.

What is offered here would waken human souls and guide them out of gloomy vaults and moldy catacombs to the experience of their spiritual *resurrection*.

But many are whose souls lie buried, who do not even realize they live entombed in crypts amidst decay and putrefaction.

Others unawares descend ever more deeply into spheres of night and death because they let themselves be lured by the desire to examine, as closely as possible, the ghostly phosphorescence of decay, until they can no longer find an exit that might lead them back into the light of day.

It thus is necessary that a brightly glowing torch will clearly show to those in danger by what they are surrounded.

Likewise, there is need to warn the unsuspecting that the hidden "temples" they believed to have discovered and were drawn to enter are in truth the chambers of the dead.

But now no more of figurative language.

The meaning and intention of this book will be quite clear in any case to every reader free of prejudice; likewise, one will understand why the various chapters, each complete in itself, appear in their given sequence.

No reader who absorbed this book as it is meant to be absorbed is likely to regret the choice of having done so. Indeed, I think such readers then will many times examine it again, until the day when they awaken to attain that *Resurrection* which neither is a miracle past comprehension, nor a gift of arbitrary grace, but—

every human being's Spirit-given calling.

Bô Yin Râ

CHAPTER ONE

RESURRECTION

I NDEED, THERE ARE ETERNALLY unchanging, timeless truths that shine like everlasting stars into the darkness veiling human beings' lives on this earth; truths that would remind them in their exile far from God of the primordial light from which they are themselves descended according to their spiritual essence.

Blest are they who, yoked to earthly toil and burdens, still have the strength to lift their eyes to those transcendent, otherworldly heights from which such wondrous light may reach them, that its eternal splendor may imbue their hearts.

All earthly gloom departs from those who journey through life's darkness in that radiance; and where ghostly phantoms once had filled their hearts with fear, there now shall angels guide them on their path to light.

But burdened by this life's relentless needs, many lost the courage to raise their eyes beyond the earth; and so they fear the ground beneath their feet might crumble if ever they feel any longing deep within to lift their heads and look above.

They hear voices shouting in their ears,

"You are no more than thralls in bondage to the earth, whose chains you cannot break.

"Dismiss the dream that help might ever reach you from a higher realm of light!

"Do not believe the vain conceits that seek to tell you of a kingdom of the Spirit, which was invented merely by misguided weaklings, who, like yourselves, were forced to trudge through thorny wastelands, and sought to make themselves forget the festering blisters of their bleeding feet by dreaming up such fairy tales."

Not a few allowed the strident croaking of such voices to dishearten them; and as they dare no longer hope that help might reach them from above their days on earth become no more than suffering in darkness and sacrifices lacking sense.

Yet even they could have been liberated by the Spirit's light, and thus would soon have found the darkness all around them brightly lit, if only they had opened themselves to receive the rays of light that sought to reach them from the Spirit's realm.

Long ago there had lived one who was entrusted with a "mission" by his "Father," of whom he spoke as being "greater" than he was himself, and who had said,

> "I am the Resurrection and the Life; he
> that believes in me shall live, though
> he were dead; and no one who believes
> in me shall die in all eternity."

And here he clearly did not speak about a rigid mental creed but of *himself* and of his timeless *spiritual individuation*; nor left he any doubt when saying that he "knew *his own*," and that "*his own* knew him."

Yet most today still have no inkling who he truly was that had authority to speak these words; nor who those were whom he regarded as *his own*; nor who the *Father* was whose *mission* he performed.

The world has not yet probed the depth of the foundation that underlies his saying,

> "Whoever does not love me does not obey my word; and the word you hear me speaking is not mine, but of the Father who sent me."

His very life, however, was his "teaching"; and in his person he embodied the answer to every mystery surrounding mortal man's existence on this earth.

But only those whose love embraces that which here was manifested in material form are able to experience in themselves the essence of that answer.

HE, THE PUREST vessel of primordial love that ever has been born on earth, is even now a living presence, in his immortal body, in the earth's protective spiritual aura. Yet he, whom timeless love keeps near the earth "until the end of the world," cannot reveal himself except to those who will receive him in their hearts through love.

Those, however, in whose hearts he thus reveals himself, will certainly no longer doubt that now they, too, have gained their *resurrection*, even as the radiant Master once had gained it when his timeless work of love on earth had been completed.

IGNORE ALL DOUBTS that needless learning raises, seeking to becloud the radiant light of truth transmitted to you in the ancient sacred writings.

Admittedly, these texts have come into our hands only after more than one redactor had wanted them to prove his own misguided notions, and thus had rearranged the words accordingly to that effect; because those writers' narrow thinking could not grasp what others, who indeed had known the truth, endeavored to convey in these reports.

Forgive those unenlightened minds what they have done and set out on your own to find the guiding thread that leads you back to the original truth that once had been recorded in these writings.

More than a few passages may thus reveal themselves as later scribes' inventions; but in this way the radiant light of truth, which nonetheless remains embodied in the ancient text, will reach your hearts the more abundantly.

You thus will surely recognize that his material body could no longer serve the resurrected Master; yet then you shall perceive his spiritual resurrection with only greater clarity, until you one day shall experience in yourselves the testimony of the one who rose above the bondage of this earth.

I myself am able to bear witness both of him, and of his spiritual resurrection, as surely as I could of the existence of the sun; and anyone acquainted with me also knows that I am not to be included among the thralls of their deceptive dreams, nor those enchained by fanciful illusions.

Even so, I do not wish that readers should believe what I affirm before they have within themselves experienced that my words convey the truth.

I merely seek to show all those who in the present darkness earnestly desire inner light how they may find the way that once again will let them reach the light of Truth, whose rays had long ago illuminated this mortal life's enigmas for the ancients, who had sought it in simplicity of spirit, unhindered by the obstacles to faith which burden mortals of the present age.

To THOUSANDS I already have been able to bring help, but thousands more lie even now still fast asleep and hunger anxiously in frightening dreams for their awakening.

Many still do not yet know that they are able to gain certainty of final knowledge *on their own*, and then shall in themselves behold a wonder surpassing every miracle that human thirst for things miraculous has ever prompted mortals to believe.

Their spiritual awakening is the end my words are meant to serve, so that the truth may one day manifest itself to all: the Truth about the Resurrection of the "Son of Man."

Those who are not able to experience it within themselves will all their lives regard it merely as a pious legend, or treat it as an article of faith.

They scarcely will be able to imagine that the ancients' thirst for miracles had made them bold enough to represent as a material, physical occurrence what in reality had been a purely spiritual event upon the highest plane.

Not until they have themselves been "resurrected" shall they behold the truth that lay behind the symbols of the imagery.

CHAPTER TWO

THE KNOWLEDGE OF SAGES

A SAGE ENDOWED WITH TIMELESS wisdom as a rule possesses little of what in earthly life is prized as "knowledge."

He, instead, is conscious of a kind of knowing that remains unknown and inexplicable to many who on earth regard themselves as having "knowledge."

But based upon his way of knowing, the sage knows with objective certainty that many a thing that mortal understanding looks upon as "knowledge" in fact is only hanging from a spider's flimsy web and ceases to be "true" and "accurate" the instant when this thread is torn.

RESURRECTION

And tear it one day surely will for each and every mortal.

Yet those who then surround the lifeless form of the departed will seek in vain to grasp that someone, who the day before had been alive as they still are, has found the very thread from which their own entire earthly knowledge still seems to hang so very firmly—to have been permanently severed.

They cannot fathom that for him, who left his earthly shell behind, the whole of what is still suspended from their spider's web, for them, has been forever torn away; hurled into the bottomless abyss, whose river of oblivion carries it away, like everything consumed by usage and decay once it has served its purpose.

Although he left the earth behind, he nonetheless continues to desire knowledge as he did before; but since all things he used to know have now deserted him forever, he seeks instead a different kind of knowledge: one that is not hanging merely on a flimsy thread, having value only while the cobweb is not cut.

However, it will not be of much use to him to seek that lasting kind of knowledge as long as he stays blinded by the way of knowing he has lost, of which he once had been so very sure.

He will profit very little by searching for the new, eternal kind of knowing in the way he used to gain his knowledge here on earth.

Because the knowledge thus attained again will only be suspended from a flimsy web, as were the matters he had known before; and even though such knowledge may appear secure for infinitely longer ages, one day that thread as well is bound to break.

Human beings, therefore, benefit by recognizing, already here on earth, that all the knowledge gained by thought and mental speculation is merely hanging like a dewdrop from the cobweb that the spider "intellection" gets to spin between the things that are *no more*, and those which are *not yet*.

Having comprehended that reality, they will no longer trust such knowing absolutely, even though they prudently may use the power and control such knowledge grants them here on earth in mastering this mortal life.

The intuition of a different kind of knowing shall awaken in them like a sprouting seed; a kind of knowledge that will not *de-pend* upon the spider web connecting the *no more* and the *not yet*.

If then one day the cobweb breaks from which their earthly knowledge was suspended, they will be found prepared to gain that other kind of knowing, whose fundaments are anchored in the deepest Ground of Being.

THAT VERY KNOWLEDGE, truly, is the wisdom that a sage possesses, even in his life on earth; and no one should regard himself as wise who has not also found it.

Knowing in that way is how one comes to knowledge in eternal realms, such as one day all shall get to know it, even if they needed aeons before they will be able to transcend the confines of contingent knowledge.

All knowledge that is gained on earth remains outside its object. *Knowing* in eternity, however, unifies the one pursuing knowledge, the object of his knowing, and the knowledge generated in a state of perfect oneness.

Only in this way one truly *knows*.

CHAPTER THREE

EFFECTS OF LAW AND CHANCE

Is it pure "chance," my friend, that you this day have come to read these words, or do you think some "law" must be at work to make this juncture possible?

Your answer will be strongly influenced, I have no doubt, by the direction of the paths you laid down for your thinking, so that it might detect a passage through the jungle of this earthly life's events.

You thus perhaps will tell me that, in your opinion, "chance" is merely the effect of hidden orders of causality; but then again, your answer might be also that you do not in the least assume some law to be involved in this.

Either answer can be justified by reasons; but final certainty will even so elude you.

But certainty you here should truly strive to gain if you would ever learn correctly to evaluate events unfolding in your life.

May such certainty arise within you through my words!

What first must here be touched upon is doubtless quite familiar; however, there is need above all else for clarity concerning what we want the terms of "law" and "chance" to signify between us.

You think that "law" is secretly at work or, in your judgment, may be clearly seen in every chain of physical events in which from an effect you can deduce its cause, or where you can anticipate a given cause will bring about a known effect.

On the other hand, when you encounter an effect you also could imagine being otherwise, given that its cause is hidden from your sight, you call the outcome "chance."

To be sure, you clearly can detect a cause accounting for the fact these words have reached you at this time; indeed, a veritable chain of causal links comes into view, the last of which, and closest to yourself, led to your reading them this moment.

Yet all the tracing back of links connecting past events will only show you that nothing happens here on earth that could be isolated from the chain of cause and consequences.

I<small>N VAIN YOU</small> search for any gap where you might possibly espy a sign of "chance."

Cause is followed by effect, which then in turn becomes the cause producing new effects; however, at no point can you detect the lever, which frequently deflects this linkage, as observation amply demonstrates, in ways apparently so arbitrary that by resorting to the concept "chance" you purposely avoid admitting to yourself how insufficient for obtaining clarity in this regard the tools at your disposal truly are.

Y<small>OU SEARCH IN</small> vain; for what you seek is hidden from your ways of seeking.

You search in vain; for what you hope to find can never be discovered where you think it may be found.

RESURRECTION

Everything that you ascribe to "chance" is in reality an element that—as the concept's etymology explains—has chanced to "fall" into the causal sequence of events as an "addition," originating in the world's invisible dimension, which to you is not accessible; unless, that is, you merely speak of "chance" from superstition, or to have a ready pseudo-answer for things you are not able to explain.

While "law" as such is not annulled wherever "chance" comes into play, there now appears a different, additional chain of cause and consequence, but interwoven with the sequence of events unfolding in external life, whose nature you are able to observe and trace. Now as this second chain asserts its influence, the individual concatenations of external forces are often made to intersect each others' paths in ways that differ markedly from what would have been necessary in the absence of such influence.

What you regard as "chance" is nothing other than the visible effect of what to you are unknown influences from the world's invisible dimension.

EFFECTS OF LAW AND CHANCE

These influences can derive from widely differing sources. They may have been initiated by entities of the invisible domain of nature, which is hidden from your senses; by human beings living on this earth like you; or by the will of timeless spiritual powers.

In every instance of authentic "chance," however, one needs to look for such an impulse as its cause; an influence proceeding from a sphere of action that your mortal senses cannot apprehend.

"Chance" as well is subject to established rules of action, but the laws that govern it are not confined to those that human mental observation is able to survey and probe.

"Chance" results from interweaving of the given laws that govern the external world with those of the unknown domain of nature, which earthly senses cannot grasp; it is always brought about, however, by an act of conscious will.

Whether such an impulse may affect you in a beneficial or destructive way depends upon its authors, who are hidden from your sight.

Behind each genuine "chance," however, you may detect an active will that normally is lacking in events; nor ought you to regard as "chance" whatever may occur unless you clearly recognize that kind of will involved in the occurrence.

Perhaps, my friend, you now are better able to answer the question I had asked at the beginning; be it that you here see nothing other than the automatic sequence of mere physical events, or that you may feel justified to speak of it as an authentic "chance"?

At least you can no longer harbor any doubts concerning what your answer ought to be.

But since I raised the question merely for the sake of the example, you will concede that your response is here not of importance.

Not unimportant for yourself will be, however, that you learn from now on to pay close attention to the "chances" that befall your life.

They offer you the only signs that let you draw conclusions as to the nature of the influences that may reach your life on earth from the dimensions hidden from your sight.

If, following your will's resolve, you are pursuing questionable goals, you will observe that "chance," directed by the lowest entities of nature's unseen realm shall soon facilitate your path toward evil deeds that lead to guilt, and every day you will be facing new temptations that you did not seek.

On the other hand, if you already found the way into the Spirit, you here as well shall meet with "chance" at every step; but now it is directed by the Spirit's guides from highest realms of love, who thus are able to bring much within your reach that you have need of for your spiritual unfolding on your path through this external world.

Every encounter with "chance" confronts you with an unexpected test, which will reveal the side you choose, by either your rejection or acceptance of what it seeks to offer.

EVEN WHERE YOU find that "chance" had worked as your protector, and only later recognize how much you are its debtor, you will be able to confirm your inner worth—by not merely taking the event for granted, but by letting it become a useful lesson.

RESURRECTION

The more attention you will pay to "chance" whenever you encounter it, the greater will become its value in your life.

The more effectively you use what "chance" may have to offer you, the richer benefits you can expect to gather from that source.

What the course of automatic causal "law" would never show as predetermined in your fate, may come into your life by "chance."

May "chance" enrich your life with many blessings!

CHAPTER FOUR

WASTED LABORS

There are many nowadays who have become aware that every content they had sought to give their lives provided merely temporary satisfaction.

And so they now are searching for a different content, one that never can be lost, and they intuitively sense that this enduring content must somehow be accessible; indeed, that others had been able to attain it, in every age and region, and even under life's most difficult conditions.

It certainly is pardonable to believe that the desired content one can never lose may only be acquired in the same way as all other things one has been able to attain on earth.

RESURRECTION

One thus assumes it merely is a question of once again exhuming some forgotten secret knowledge; and so it is mistakenly believed that one would readily possess the longed-for content of one's life if but the hidden things were known, which had apparently been found by those whose lives were guided by that content.

Cause and effect are here unwittingly confused; for the desired content, to be sure, would lead one also to new knowledge, but never could its essence be transmitted by the things of which one merely knows.

Therefore it is truly wasted labor if seekers will set out to scour antiquarian book stores to examine esoteric ruminations of the past, or let themselves become the willing dupes of every mystagogue of modern times who is deluded by the phantoms of his all too earthly thinking—all in the erroneous belief that the enduring knowledge, which only *transformation of one's will* can grant, may be attained the same way as the understanding of the things we know on earth.

Countless groups and sects came into being as a result of seekers' thirst to rediscover the envisioned timeless content of this life.

Credulous enthusiasts, mentally unfettered dreamers, but also outright swindlers have come into positions of importance in these circles that elsewhere in the world they never would have gained.

Time and again the feeble hope that in the end one still might find what one is seeking draws new disciples to these groups; and the assurances of so-called "gurus" effectively keep many seekers in the fold, despite the fact their common sense has long since told them that they surely could more usefully employ their energy, their leisure, and their money.

Wasted labor is the expectation that one's life's enduring content could ever be discovered in circles of that kind.

Many, for a time at least, may thus be led astray; and there are some whose final remnant of self-criticism may be swept away by torrents of imposing words, so that they are no longer able to recognize how grossly they deceive themselves.

Their "guru's" attitude of unapproachable aloofness becomes their surest proof of "truth."

In vain, however, shall one look for even one among both "guides" and their misguided flock who actually attained the final certainty that truly stills the longing for the timeless content of existence all are seeking.

I MAY WITHOUT exaggeration say there is no circle of the kind to which I here refer, whatever names they choose to give themselves, from which profoundly disillusioned members had not come to me lamenting their experience.

Volumes could be filled if one intended to record all things these victims told me of the harm they suffered.

More than once I was reluctant to believe what I was told, until I was shown documents that even went beyond what I had heard.

How is it possible, I asked myself, that educated people, some even holding university degrees in science, are capable of falling prey to such egregious flummery, to such unconscionable fishing after human souls?

And with embarrassment the victims would admit that they for years had seen through the deception, but could not find the courage to confess to others, who quickly had discerned it, as outsiders, that they had for so long allowed themselves to be misguided by the error of their fellow seekers, or the brazen posture of allegedly "initiated" guides.

Shocking examples of breakdowns came to my attention; and horrified I had to see the dreadful consequences set in motion, on the one hand by credulity that knows no bounds, and on the other, by a degree of irresponsibility one only could explain as self-deception.

But not from groups like these alone come disappointed souls who, after years of fruitless seeking, finally discerned, in resignation, how much they had deceived themselves.

There also are some other ways to lose one's labor and to drift each day still farther from the goal that is desired, while feeling sure one is approaching it in giant strides.

All of that I have sufficiently discussed and warned against in other books.

Far too inconspicuous, too lacking in the mystifying thrill of "magic," do many find the strait and narrow path on which alone the goal desired can be reached.

But in addition, I would here still mention a particularly foolish way in which too many waste their energy, their time and money, driven from one disappointed hope to yet another, until at last they are compelled to face the painful sobering truth.

The waste I have in mind is the voracious, indiscriminate devouring of all books and booklets that somehow touch upon the sphere of the "occult," or merely by their titles promise "insights" into hidden matters.

However, this is not to give the false impression that I consider reading all works dealing with that topic as potentially inviting harm.

But I doubt that anyone sufficiently familiar with the field is likely to dispute my claim that in no other area of literature is one confronted with so much, and such explicit, rubbish as in the publications dealing with phenomena of the occult.

The subject matter itself accounts for this condition.

It is a field concerning which there always have been only few, in any age, who competently could disclose the truth, while at the same time countless others have, in every generation, abundantly spun fantasies from their abstruse illusions.

The danger here lies in the fact that only those who can objectively distinguish are able to determine where things discussed still rest on solid ground, although it often may be hard to see, and where, by contrast, one is faced with fairy tales of the absurd.

A further danger is the fact that countless publications in that field are nothing more than repetitions drawn from four or five related books on things occult, thereby creating the appearance of established proof, a snare that often will entrap the novice.

A third related danger I see in the practice of some otherwise noteworthy authors, who surely are entitled to present the findings of their personal speculation, but, thoroughly convinced by the correctness of their views, will then adopt a tone in writing that easily may cause the reader to believe that he is being told about unshakably established insights into the profoundest depth of Being, although these are at any time accessible to only very few.

Anyone acquainted with publications in the field of the occult will find it easy to recognize examples for everything I here describe as harmful.

Yet seekers buy and keep on buying, perhaps in every pocket carrying a pamphlet they revere like holy writ.

Enormous libraries will be collected in this way, and every inkling of dissatisfied uneasiness is promptly stifled by the acquisition of yet another worthless tome.

But let us for the moment actually accept that each and every one of these innumerable publications, which frequently exude the odor of commercialism at its worst, contained in fact the purest truth.

Their contents then might possibly provide material for research of more or less significance, and in this way they could expand their readers' learning.

Readers even could perhaps discover hints as to the way they should pursue their search for life's enduring content, so that they one day will indeed attain the object of their quest.

Yet whatever they may learn about unknown activities and facts concerning the occult— assuming all of it were purest truth—it may at best enrich their minds, but never could it grant them the desired content itself that still is missing in their lives.

That enduring content is transmitted only through the guidance of the few that have throughout the ages known about its nature, and how it is attained, and who are therefore able to show the way that leads to its attainment.

The content sought, however, can be found by everyone, no matter whether he believes himself informed in all details of occultism, or rather waits in patient reverence before enigmas still unknown until they shall reveal themselves, by nature's laws.

At the very least one ought to bear in mind that all attempts to penetrate the workings of mysterious realities are beneficial only if this leads to heightened reverence for what continues to be hidden.

The essential facts that human beings need to learn about are only those particular relationships that may inspire them to structure their own lives in such a way that they become accessible, at last, to inner help from the dimension of the Spirit, which raises them, already in their earthly lives, to the awakened consciousness of their eternal nature.

THIS ETERNAL consciousness unlocks not merely a *new content*, but is at once a new and different way of *being conscious*.

Nothing then can any longer reach the human being from without; and once this state of *consciousness-in-being* is attained, all knowledge henceforth is confirmed within.

Even teaching then no longer serves a purpose; for everything it once had needed to convey through words has now become reality that is forever present, and consciously discerned at will.

The intuitively sensed, so ardently desired content of one's life has been attained forever.

Wasted labor was the effort to acquire it through thought!

Wasted labor the attempt to search for it in dusty tomes!

Wasted labor the belief in teachers who in blindness lead the blind!

Wasted labor, finally, had been the effort to gain the lasting content of one's life, which is a new experience of *being conscious*, by seeking to increase one's knowledge of the mysteries behind the things that nature keeps concealed from our eyes; knowledge that reverts to nothing the moment when our earthly body's senses at last must end their service.

CHAPTER FIVE

MARDI GRAS OF THE OCCULT

The peculiar pleasure of hiding behind a mask and in disguise to play all sorts of pranks is given license, as one knows, to have its way without restraint at a specific season once a year; and where this custom is observed with wit and in good humor, one gladly will observe the revels as they pass, even if one does not feel the slightest inclination to take part in the parade.

After all, the time allotted to this merriment is brief; nor is there any dearth of serious days to follow.

Only when the urge to don disguises to indulge in mummery runs wild in spheres of life wherein such conduct has no business does it become a problem.

RESURRECTION

One such domain wherein the jests of carnival appear to be in season all year round is that of modern occultism; despite the many earnest seekers who with pure intent would here discover satisfying answers to the enigmas of existence.

Merely by surveying recent, or the latest publications in the field—to the extent this still is possible today, considering the flood of needless products on the subject—one cannot miss examples of the most unbridled Mardi Gras.

Yet all this patent mummery insists on being taken seriously and thus presents a danger for many who approach it.

With unbelievable impertinence one practices the most outlandish slight-of-hand and offers it to the uncritical, whose numbers never seem to dwindle, as the true, authentic art of "magic." With unsurpassed audacity the operators of this carnival display themselves in gaudy, glittering costumes and demand that one regard their tinsel as pure gold, and take their glassy beads for precious gems.

But however shopworn and transparent the postures of the trickery might be, each new gesture will unfailingly attract new converts.

If it merely were the spiritually immature, who keep on running after every harlequin who drums his rattle on his bag of tricks, claiming it contains the ultimate "philosopher's stone," one possibly might understand it. What almost seems beyond belief, however, is the fact that all too often even people let themselves be hoodwinked who elsewhere miss no opportunity to boast about their thoroughgoing skepticism.

WHERE IS THE reverence before the wisdom of the greatest sages that have walked the earth if one can be deluded to believe that some obscure adventurer might know about the mysteries whose depths to probe the wisest of the wise had labored all their lives and would reveal to only pupils who could comprehend them?

Can one seriously believe eternal wisdom has become so trivial in our day that buyers cannot be attracted unless it will be dumped like overstock at discount prices?

Are there truly minds today prepared to tolerate the notion that one is able to attain the *union of one's soul with God* by occult exercises of whatever kind? And does one hold those in such low regard who in their day had truly reached this goal that one imagines their profoundest secrets are unveiled, because some impecunious pamphlet writer claims that, being an initiate, he came to know them, in detail, and under more or less mysterious circumstances?

ONE IS OFTEN tempted to believe that any trace of basic judgment bids farewell to the majority of minds the moment they explore the realm of the "occult."

Here, everything is taken at face value, which would at once be recognized as counterfeit if one did not naively trust the self-promoting bluster of those who try to sell their brass as solid gold.

Credulity appears to have no bounds, especially if the presumed "initiate" will skillfully deflect all questions touching his own character by means of lofty words he took from others.

MARDI GRAS OF THE OCCULT

If, furthermore, he will give the impression of expertise in many fields, suggesting to the uninformed that here they face a master of all knowledge, then such a charlatan can hazard almost anything without the risk of having his deceit unmasked.

A WELL-STOCKED box of index cards, together with a sizable collection of tracts on occult lore, both old and new, is often the entire arsenal of the pretended knowledge of such a pettifogger; and only his disciples' unawareness of dubious publications of that sort protects him from discovery.

There is no need to single out particularly entertaining jests that flourish in the occult Mardi Gras.

Whoever will observe this carnival hilarity with open eyes and is not overawed by daring acrobatics shall find examples at discretion; and if he feels inclined he well may recognize whole categories of repeatedly recurring Mardi Gras disguises.

The most exotic characters he may encounter in this masquerade; and if he has not lost his sense of humor, a hearty laugh will more than once relieve his natural indignation.

But shame and pity for the human being's sake are bound to sadden the observer when in the midst of this grotesque commotion he watches those who actually believe in the disguises they adopted and can no longer recognize that they are wearing masks.

The more one learns to see through all the glittering costumes, which some parade in solemn gravity, while others make them sparkle by their fancy leaps, the less one feels desire for such company.

Here we find the perfect playground of all who were derailed in their existence; and more than one who, in his ludicrously trimmed magician's robe, now plays his shopworn, wretched part had only come to choose that role since he had failed in life and, facing imminent collapse, sought refuge in the realm of the occult.

For those entrapped in this dilemma, however, necessity brooks no constraints; and even if at first they did not dream of actually believing in the things their costumes represented, the pressure of their situation gradually compelled them to appear imbued with faith, a challenge they accomplish with consummate skill.

After all, a mask will only be effective at a proper Mardi Gras if it successfully conceals its bearer.

W<small>ERE IT NOT</small> that all too often honest seekers are bewildered by this travesty, one simply might ignore it and move on.

But human souls are here in peril; and even if for most of them, who sometimes fail for years to recognize they had indulged in a perpetual carnival, a sobering Ash Wednesday is ultimately bound to dawn, the bitter knowledge of having wasted precious time remains a constant obstacle; despite the fact they later may pursue the only path that leads to the attainment of the goal they had originally longed to reach.

They now must time and again admit to themselves that if they were deceived the fault was theirs alone; for no one here is free of guilt who let his judgment be so paralyzed that he was able to mistake this masquerade for the authentic path to truth.

Whoever in external life believes each promising advertisement without first making sure that the promoter can be trusted, should not complain if in addition to his loss he also will reap mockery.

How much more consequential, then, becomes the duty carefully to choose before one trusts, if on such trust depends the bliss or desolation of the soul that longs for light and clarity!

One surely need not be endowed with singular intelligence to comprehend that God's eternal Spirit, which is to unify itself with the awakened spirit of the human self, cannot be tricked into this union by means of "methods" one can learn from merchandisers selling occult "secrets."

It simply is such trickery, however, that all things in the end amount to in the various, for the most part purely physical, "exercises" offered to their followers by any of the carnival magicians, who are but sorry imitations of blessed Count Cagliostro.

Thus it clearly is the aim to get by devious means what one believes too difficult to reach in honest ways that never fails to lure new victims into the nets of vain impostors.

It likewise is the craving to experience signs and wonders that leads to this result; but here one disregards completely that even the most wondrous of mysterious events that mortal senses can perceive no longer has the slightest worth the moment when these senses must forgo their service.

WHOEVER WILL NOT cast aside all things that veil his timeless self—wherein he shall unendingly abide in Being, in God's eternal Spirit—and hide that self from his mere earthly consciousness cannot attain the union with his living God.

How, then, could any mortal ever hope to bring about that union, which is to last through all eternity, if in addition he festoons himself in carnival apparel of all kinds?

RESURRECTION

He thus awakens only forces that so effectively will bar his path to God that it becomes impassable to him; for only those who truly are united with their God, are capable, by virtue of the Spirit's might, to master the demonic forces, which fools awaken only from their sleep in the belief that with their help they will ascend to godlike wisdom.

Only unsuspecting ignorance can casually dismiss the fact that powers of that kind exist.

But those who clearly see the world with open eyes will all too often recognize the traces of their ruinous activity.

Consummate masters of disguises of all kinds, they lastly are the unseen puppeteers who pull the strings to move the marionettes which populate the occult Mardi Gras.

CHAPTER SIX

INNER VOICES

A LREADY MANKIND'S OLDEST RECORDS on this planet tell of individuals who, at certain times, in certain places, and under certain circumstances, would hear "voices" speak to them that no one else could hear; and according to the level of their inner knowledge and the images of their religious faith, they would interpret what these voices said.

For the listener there is no question that the voice that speaks to him proceeds from some external entity he very clearly can distinguish from himself.

Most definitely he would reject the intimation that he was merely speaking to himself and thus transforming his ideas into a personal dramatic "dialogue." To be sure, there also will be those who in this manner inwardly address themselves, yet are convinced of being guided by some higher spiritual being.

Objective judgment here is only gained through personal experience; much as expert knowledge in the arts is not attained by merely theoretical instruction, but rather by sufficient practice in the field.

Whoever has repeatedly heard real inner voices can no longer be deceived by self-induced interior monologues.

FAR MORE DIFFICULT than making this distinction is gaining needed certainty concerning the originators of such inner voices.

Credulity is here all too inclined to trust they emanate from highest spiritual authority, especially when knowledge still is lacking that unseen entities of the most varied kinds exist which in effect can manifest themselves as inner voices.

Individuals so utterly devoid of pride and arrogance that they appear oppressed by feelings of imagined inferiority, then suddenly become transformed into the perfect opposite; for now they see themselves as "tools of God" and overbearingly demand respect of all the world because of their assumed "elected grace," quite unaware that by their very conduct they convincingly exhibit the deceptive nature of the inner voices which have gained their trust.

Again and again one can observe that even deeply skeptical natures will throw all caution to the wind the moment they themselves experience things the possibility of which they once had so complacently rejected.

Whatever now that inner voice may say, they trustingly believe; and most unquestionably it is believed if it presents itself as coming from a higher spiritual being, the loftier the better, if not indeed as that of God himself.

If, in addition, the listener hears a message that he is chosen to perform a saintly mission and ought to see himself as one of the "elect," in order to enrich the world with an especial blessing, then every inclination henceforth to have doubts about that voice is permanently stifled; even though the only fact established at this point is the intrusion of an inner voice, but without any proof it truly is the one it claims to be.

Objectively considered, anyone who hears an inner voice is not unlike a person who receives a phone call from a stranger.

The caller may be no more than a lowly swindler and yet present himself as holding fancy titles and degrees, because he knows full well his chances of succeeding in his criminal design depend on passing as a personality that will inspire confidence in the receiver of his call.

But who on earth, except an outright fool, would ever undertake a consequential task merely at the bidding of a caller on the phone?

Would not anyone with but a shred of common sense seek first of all to get some proof before considering to undertake a task imposed upon him by an unknown voice?

Similarly, anyone who hears an inner voice is being prompted by an unseen caller; nor has he any means of verifying whether what is stated rests on truth; unless, that is, he has already been informed about some typical criteria that instantly unmask all efforts to deceive.

The following will briefly summarize the most important of these telling signs.

FIRST. WHOEVER THINKS he hears a voice that speaks to him within, and which he feels as coming from an unseen source he clearly can distinguish from himself, should bear in mind that there are countless unseen entities of the most varied natures, which are able, under specific conditions, to manifest themselves as speaking inner voices; and, further, that by far the largest part of the invisible intruders who can be heard most easily are of the suspect kind, so that he should make every effort not to attract their influence.

Very seldom will a truly *spiritual* being—one by nature of a higher level in the Spirit than are mortal humans—"speak" within a person's self; and where this rare event occurs in truth, it only is made possible by the advanced degree of spiritual development the one addressed already has attained.

Consequently, if one is not certain of having reached that high degree of spiritual attainment, one resolutely should reject all inner voices, no matter how seductively they try to gain the listener's trust.

SECOND. ANY "VOICE" experienced as proceeding from an unseen entity is to be ignored at once if the transmitted words are audible not only to the inner, spiritual sense, but also to the physical, external ear.

At best this situation signals a disturbance of the nervous system, which ought not to be taken lightly, so that one promptly should seek medical advice.

Far more serious, however, is the situation if the unseen entities of nature's unknown side already have succeeded in possessing their hapless human victim to the point that such voices can be heard as physically experienced sounds even when no clinical symptoms of nervous disorders can be diagnosed.

Yet in such cases nothing is accomplished by attempts to fight them; the only thing one here can do is simply to ignore them, consistently, and for extended periods.

Every place and setting is to be avoided that in the past had seemed to favor the speaking of such voices.

While it is surely possible to rid oneself at last of their intrusion, this will depend upon the victim's firm resolve in future not to pay them the slightest attention, under any circumstances, but to treat them instead like other incidental noises.

In particular, the victim must avoid all signs of showing fear, but likewise ought not to adopt the hostile attitude of someone bent to fight them.

Whatever they may tell, or even "order" the victim to do, one simply must ignore; indeed, one should not even think about the meaning of their messages.

Energetic physical work, a meaningful activity outdoors, congenial company, and, in general, avoiding solitude as far as possible, will prove effective means to rid oneself of the unwanted unseen parasites.

Whoever suffered from this infestation may count himself extremely fortunate if, by virtue of consistently ignoring the phenomena, he finally succeeded in once more being free and master of his senses.

THIRD. PROFOUND SUSPICION should at once arise when such an inner voice pronounces a command, or tells the victim it addresses about a "task" or "mission" he was chosen to fulfill in life.

Individuals who truly have a task, a mission, or something of that nature to perform in life receive their spiritual commission in a very different, expressly sober, non-mysterious manner; nor would any of them ever be found willing, merely at the prompting of an "inner voice," to undertake what those demand of them who are the Spirit's sole authentic agents here on earth.

IN SUMMARY, IT should be stressed that any inner voice should be rejected that speaks of matters other than what will advance the person's higher spiritual development, illuminate his inner understanding, and make him better as a human being.

Never shall a voice proceeding truly from the timeless realm of Spirit seek to motivate a human being to the end of influencing others in whatever form.

It solely shall assist in the unfolding of a person's spiritual love toward other human beings. In every case, however, it lets the inwardly instructed pupil freely choose how to express that love in action, according to his powers.

To be sure, authentic spiritual guidance, too, is able to assume the concrete form of spoken inner words, which then the guided person clearly hears in his respective language.

Such inner speaking, however, will always be experienced only in the inmost self—within the human being's spiritual organism—as if the unknown speaker were indeed the person's proper self; for solely through the human mortal's own eternal essence can beings that are truly of the Spirit's world communicate with humans.

As a result of the grotesque ideas concerning the occult that nowadays are everywhere confusing people's minds, a veritable thirst for hearing inner voices is created; and the phenomenon enjoys such high demand that many would experience it at any price.

It chiefly is that widespread craving which offers the lemurian parasites of nature's hidden realm their chance to make themselves important and to produce the things in such demand.

Much like parasites of visible nature, those of her unseen world as well like places best where they can thrive in squalor and decay, or in the dark of moldy corners.

Whoever would remain protected from this unseen brood should thus take care to keep his inner life of thought, imagination, and emotional drives, at all times governed by superior cleanliness.

Heeding this, one scarcely will fall victim to the hunger for sensations, which has already brought so many to the brink of mental ruin.

THOSE WHO TRULY had become prepared to hear the sound of an authentic spiritual voice, being guided by the Spirit's highest source, had never felt the slightest interest in hearing "inner voices." Instead, through many years of strictest discipline their aim had been to root out errors in themselves and to abolish personal shortcomings.

Thus, however, they attained the level at which the Spirit's timeless love was able to reveal itself within their inmost essence.

But only spiritual voices of such love will truly grant the human being lasting joy.

Only voices from that source can ever guide those seeking light to their eternal goal.

They come without demand, or being summoned, as soon as those who seek the Spirit's life are able to receive them.

The voices of the physically unseen demonic parasites of nature, on the other hand, are able to reach any human mortal, even those still at the lowest inner level.

Only turning away and totally ignoring them protects against their influence; and all should here take care in this way to secure their own protection.

All must bear in mind that no one else can shield them, and that no other being's spiritual power, however great, is capable of helping them so long as they still frivolously court the danger.

Only courage and determination consistently to shun them will here invoke the Spirit's help, wherever it is needed.

CHAPTER SEVEN

THE MAGIC EFFECT OF FEAR

M ORE NUMEROUS THAN THE BELIEVERS of all the world's religions is the flock of those, spread all around the globe, who without knowing practice magic by the force of fear.

To be sure, they do not know that they are working magic, and many do not even sense that they made fear their goddess, but all their thoughts, their words, and deeds make it unnecessary that they know how fear has paralyzed their faith.

Everywhere, of course, one hears impressive words of courage; and if one trusted the heroic posture of undaunted fortitude that many learned convincingly to master, one easily might come to the conclusion that fear of every kind is banished from the earth.

But hollow words and empty gestures are here of little weight; and those who rally courage only in despair do not in this way prove that they have conquered fear.

Many may indeed be fearless in a given setting, and yet are thralls to fear as soon as they have left the site where practice taught them to be not afraid.

Few, indeed, will not let fear possess their lives in any form.

NEARLY EVERYONE IS bound to feel afraid of something.

Even the bravest tends to pamper fear in certain ways.

Such has been human nature from ages immemorial, and this enduring heritage continues to be passed from each new generation to the next.

None should feel ashamed that fear may sometimes overcome him; that it attempts to force him to become its thrall.

What human beings ought to learn, however, is how to fend off such assaults.

Thus, the attacked should recognize that fear can harm them solely through their own inherent energy; in that it seeks to make them use the magic power they unknowingly possess in such a way that they themselves attract the harmful things they fear.

Fear never finds more vulnerable victims than in times of anguish and distress, when no one knows what evils must be faced tomorrow.

Given consequences brought about by past events will not be nullified by any might of earth or heaven; and where errors, committed in earlier actions, have sown the seeds of evil, its fruits must be endured, however one might struggle to be spared; nor does it matter whether one is able to discern the underlying causal chain, or not.

But here misled by flawed conclusions, humans now grant fear unfettered sway, unaware they thus increase a hundredfold, by their own powers, the evils they cannot escape.

All willingly surrender their innate magic energy, allowing it to serve the aims of fear; and when confronted with the consequences, they feel the gloomy faith confirmed which fear had planted in their minds.

As a result, the reign of evil never ceases; for constantly its rule is magically renewed.

The primal force of will, which could have changed things for the better long ago, is thus abused, prolonging the control of evil.

Blinded by the spell of fear, none among the many who thereby needlessly increase the spread of evil, has any longer faith in his own magic power, through which he likewise could bring evil to a halt, if only he were first resolved to rid himself of fear.

THIS STATE OF things cannot be helped until the day when each and everyone begins to recognize, as best he may, that he no longer must let fear control the power of this faith.

But even as the energies of countless individuals enthralled by fear become the cause of infinite effects, so, too, shall the collective energy of willing multitudes grow overwhelmingly effective if everyone will rid himself of fear.

Then shall evil be restricted to the bounds imposed by errors earlier committed, nor will it be conceded further growth.

The energy of faith at work within the many that have freed themselves of fear will now exclusively attract the good; even as the very power—chained by fear—had in the past attracted only evil.

Much lies dormant in the realm of the potential that never can become reality unless the force of human faith will bring it into being.

Evil and blessings alike are in this way brought forth.

It is no idle play with empty words if here I warn against the magic effect of fear.

Although the concept "magic" has nowadays become a shallow platitude, it is a word one nonetheless must use when speaking of the things I here discuss.

The ancients, who still knew about the magic potential of faith in mortal man from practical experience, used to distinguish between "white" and "black" in the domain of magic, depending on the beneficial or destructive consequences generated by the selfsame force.

Today one feels entitled condescendingly to smile about the ancients' "superstition," as their insights now are called; yet even to this day there is no human being on this earth who does not cause—by all his thoughts, and words, and actions, day after day, and every single hour—magical energies to work their way, affecting both himself and those who live around him.

But humans nowadays no longer know about their inner power and thus dismiss as "ineffective" what in reality initiates—everywhere and at all times—profoundly serious consequences.

One searches for the cause of evil solely in the outer world and only takes the mechanism of material events into account, while at the same time dragging evil into physical existence by one's own inherent power, through the magic force of fear, which just as surely will attract the evil that is feared, as joyous confidence, defying all external gloom, is bound to bring about the good that is desired.

Very few today still know from personal experience that this is how things work; and those who do will have no doubt that what I say is true.

They know about the magic force of confidence, having long since practiced it, replacing that of fear, often having suffered much before they saw the light.

The magic potential of confidence is needed more today than ever, and it alone is able to defeat the magic force of fear.

It cannot be denied that in the course of earthly life we may encounter much that is extremely undesirable, things we gladly would keep far away.

Nor can it be denied that fear at times may save us from committing errors, in that it calls up images of the destructive consequences of mistakes.

Fear may teach how evil is avoided and thus becomes a factor that protects and furthers life.

Only when it stirs up images of all sorts of events that well may never happen, or possibly are unavoidable, will fear become—by means of human faith—a force attracting evil.

Fear can never teach how to avoid what is inevitable, which has to be endured before it will disintegrate.

Never will inevitable evil be diminished by already fearing an impending threat.

Fear in this case merely undermines the strength we need to bear what cannot be avoided so that it will not crush us altogether.

On the other hand, what well might be avoided, yet nonetheless is feared, may all too easily become, through the magic effect of fear, an ill that cannot be escaped.

STILL, ALL THE magic force of confidence will not prevent an evil one no longer can avoid.

Its benefits lie rather in not letting evil that may be avoided cross the line from the potential sphere into the realm of fact; that it deflects much harm that seems already imminent, but will instead magnetically attract what is desired.

THE MAGIC EFFECT OF FEAR

Never is the need for confidence more urgent than at times of anxiousness and worry.

Yet precisely at such times it also gives the surest proof of its effectiveness.

Only one must not assume that human will can dictate how this power is to work.

Efficiently its lever always moves the weight where it is lifted with the least exertion.

Even when a human being does not know, and has no way of knowing, whether any chance of help may still exist, the magic force of confidence will offer him that help.

Thousands already have discovered its effect through personal experience, but hundreds of thousands still are unaware that such a power rests within the human being.

Yet all who here put to the test the things that can be tested give hope that others, too, will dare to test them on their own; and thus they will support this planet's unseen helpers in liberating other human beings from the magic yoke of fear.

RESURRECTION

Even as the force of fear had once destroyed the human spirit's cosmic freedom, as fear had been the cause of mankind's "fall" from radiant light in God, so also is the human being's mortal life relentlessly besieged by fear.

Each and everyone who helps in some degree to drive the sense of constant fear from human hearts is taking part in the eternal work of liberation.

Yet being free of fear is anything but blindness in the face of danger!

Only those who know the full extent of an impending threat are able to confront it without fear; for they alone know also how to meet it.

CHAPTER EIGHT

THE LIMITS OF OMNIPOTENCE

Among the most immovably established articles of faith, embraced by every mortal who believes in God, however widely such beliefs may differ from traditional creeds, has always been the proposition that God, in his relation to all the works proceeding from his will, remains "almighty."

A "God" without "omnipotence," typically imagined in quite earthly terms, appears to be defective, in believers' minds, of the most fundamental attribute of Godhead. Indeed, the human being will more readily invest the God of his belief with all the cruel instincts found in his own animal nature, than ever doubt the totally unlimited almightiness of God.

Anthropomorphic thinking has mentally construed a "God," who is not comprehended as the Ground of Being, transcending every individuation, but instead regarded, in more or less exaggerated form, as no more than the "highest being"; and so one logically concludes this "highest" being must of necessity be master also of "almighty" power; for otherwise it could not be regarded as the "highest" being.

Resorting to the most unconscionable sophistry one labors to ignore the fact that any such "almighty" God—in the true sense of the word, having all things in his power—would have to be a veritable monster if he could calmly tolerate all the distress and suffering, all the horrors and atrocities on earth, given that he holds the power simply to eliminate and to prevent the like.

Only when some catastrophic fate has struck them, and they feel unjustly made to suffer, will humans sometimes recognize the glaring contradiction in their view of God.

Yet far from any insight that this contradiction was their own invention, devoid of

THE LIMITS OF OMNIPOTENCE

any correspondence in reality, believers now will rail against the fiendishly sadistic idol they invented, unless they choose the radical solution henceforth to reject all faith in God —all trust in any spiritual order watching over humankind—as merely foolish self-deception.

No SINGLE DAY goes by in life on earth on which in countless places human beings do not quarrel with the God of their imagination, because they feel he burdened them with ills and anguish hard to bear.

Only with concealed resistance or embittered, fear-beclouded faith will people yet accept the shallow comfort which sundry teachers of religion still have the nerve to offer them in that they reinterpret an oppressive fate, imposed on them "according to God's undiscoverable counsel," as an expression of his favor:

"God will chastise those he loves."

Few are conscious of the flagrant blasphemy inherent in such comfort.

A HORRIBLE "GOD," indeed, who knows no better way to show his love! But then again, it is a "God" existing purely by the grace of human minds; a "God" not found within the universe of matter, nor in the Spirit's worlds, but solely in the thoughts of mortal human brains.

One certainly can understand that people in profound distress would rather look on all disclosures of divine, eternal things as fantasies, as frauds, and idle dreams than willingly continue to accept a "God" who torments those he "loves."

How very different, indeed, from such a "God" of anthropomorphic imagination is the reality encountered in the spiritual realm!

The one and only element within the creedal concept corresponding to reality remains the truth that "God is love," and that all those who will "abide in love, abide in God, and God in them."

The radiance of the Godhead's timeless light dissolves the phantom God one has endowed with crude material omnipotence, even as the rising sun dissolves the drifting vapors on a swamp.

THE LIMITS OF OMNIPOTENCE

The absolute, primordial Ground of Being, to which alone the name of God is worthy to be given, is indivisible and one within itself, even though it manifests its Essence in forms of limitless infinity.

How could it ever contradict, negate itself in any of the forms that manifest its Being?

Nothing exists within the universe that in the end is not a form that manifests primordial Being—abiding in itself as love—eternally encircled, as it were, by the forever moving energies that generate existence.

Unto itself is this primordial Being eternal "law" and "norm"; and all the infinitely varied energies that serve its manifested forms, notwithstanding their expulsion as realities in opposition, remain eternally sustained exclusively in its own Being; nor could they ever generate "existence"—phenomena in opposition—but for the power of primordial Being.

Each and every energy is, therefore, ultimately rooted in the "law" inherent in primordial Being, and thus contains its functional potential unchangeable within; even though in cosmic time, beyond the scale of human measure, the combinations of such energies that we believe to have identified as "laws of nature" are not exempt from redirection; but human observation here on earth cannot discern these changes, given it does not encompass ages so immense.

As long as any combination of such energies, which we define as "laws of nature," has not been dissolved again, primordial Being is not able to negate their function; for they as well are rooted in its very Being, and it can never abrogate Itself.

HERE ARE THE limitations of divine "omnipotence," as human minds imagine it, eternally unchangeable, even for primordial Being.

Expressed in terms of simple pious faith, this means that God would rage against himself if his volition wanted to, or could, oppose the functioning of energies effective here on earth; given that these energies derive their law and norm from the identical divine volition.

Perfection is not wanted by God's will in this dimension, nor could it here be willed;

THE LIMITS OF OMNIPOTENCE

because *perfection* only can exist in the domain of pure and absolute reality; not, however, in its opposite, which we call "physical existence."

The absolute uniqueness of primordial Being necessarily precludes the possibility that one could ever realize perfection in the realm of physical existence.

All "existence," objectively considered, is simply a "reflection" of a given aspect within the absolute primordial Being; and even as one may regard this planet's sun as "perfect" when compared to its reflected image on still water, so likewise is perfection, within primordial Being, only found in the eternal matrix of each creative energy that generates "existence," not, however, in the generated object, whose nature is experienced through perception.

To influence the world of physical perception from the dimension of God's Spirit is only possible to the extent that God's eternal will is able to affect that world without self-contradiction.

However, not the very slightest form of influence could be exerted by God's will upon this world of physical perception, if the chains of causal law that rules events were truly quite as tightly drawn as human thought likes to imagine.

But in the same way as the workings of the energy configurations, which mankind knows as laws of nature, are not by any means eternally immutable, so too are the connecting links that form the chain of causal consequences joined in ways that their direction still is relatively subject to the Spirit's will. Yet even all the spiritual power of God's will remains within the bounds of this quite relative degree to which causality can be affected; nor is it able to transgress the limits which this selfsame will encounters in itself: sanctioned by itself from all eternity.

Expressed in words of simple, heartfelt piety, one thus could say that God, indeed, is able to affect events on earth to some degree, but that his will herein restricts itself at all times to its own inherent laws; consequently, all God's influence can be exerted only by engaging the particular effectiveness of laws that function in the physical domain, laws that likewise have their source in that same timeless will.

Human beings may feel quite assured that God at all times will prevent whatever evils he is able to prevent on earth. All quarreling with God because he failed to keep some evil from occurring, therefore derives its specious "justification" simply from the foolish notion of God's material "omnipotence"—his power constantly to change all things that happen—and thus amounts to blasphemy from ignorance.

THE ABSOLUTELY changeless fact one needs to know as well, however, is that any possibility of God's diverting the direction of events of physical causality is offered solely through the intervention of the human spirit; which is to say, that any influence of God on earthly life depends upon the human being; and on that being's willingness to clear the path to that effect, whether that be done through active engagement of a person's will, or by means of passive dedication, as in prayer.

RESURRECTION

"ALL OF CREATION waits with eager longing for its liberation through the children of God."

YET EVEN HAVING knowledge of these matters one ought not to expect what is impossible, but always bear in mind that the "omnipotence" which God in truth possesses is eternally decided by the Godhead's will to manifest its Essence, and therefore cannot act in conflict with that Essence; for that, if it were possible, would equal self-annihilation.

And so there truly is "omnipotence" in God's eternal Essence, in so far as all "existence" manifests the might of this primordial Essence, not, however, in the absurd sense as if divine volition could ever have "existence," determined by itself, become determined differently from how it once, eternities ago, had been determined, in consequence of immanent necessity; given that "existence" had been set forth from the Godhead's inner realm, to be an opposite to its own Being.

Conscious efforts to keep mortal minds hypnotically subjected to the error-laden notion of an "omnipotence of God," which cannot

THE LIMITS OF OMNIPOTENCE

be, reach back into the very dawn of human history.

It truly is high time to break this mental spell, lest human beings lose all living faith in God.

Not until the limits of omnipotence are recognized can one gain understanding of the universe: as the eternal revelation of primordial might.

CHAPTER NINE

THE NEW LIFE

GREAT IS THE NUMBER OF THOSE IN our time who are searching for light.

Yet always far more numerous remains the multitude in bondage to the earth who do not feel the longing after light that stirs the souls who seek.

Unaware of their confined horizon, those enchained by physically curtailed perception thus believe that everything the human being is able to experience in this life is limited to that which they and others of their kind are capable of apprehending.

When others seek the path that leads them to the Spirit, those in fetters of their creature senses judge them to be foolish dreamers.

The faculty of thought defines their world of "spirit," and they no longer comprehend the language of their fellow mortals who intuitively fathom a reality beyond the knowledge gained by thinking.

Human thought, of course, had long ago constructed "hell" and "heaven"; however, thought was likewise also to dissolve again the constructs it had wrought. Consequently, thinking minds felt justified, based upon experience, to conclude that the transcendent goal pursued by seeking souls was likewise a "reality" contrived by merely speculation, and thus of similarly nebulous existence, and dissolvable by thought, as were the worlds their own minds had created.

And in this way the height and reach of what the human being is by nature able to perceive, regrettably remains unknown to most; for they believe that in the narrow confines of their thinking they have found the "spirit," feel secure within their mental world, and thus no longer feel the impulse to search for the primordial Spirit where alone it can be found—in the light of an *experience* that no thought can bring about.

THE NEW LIFE

THAT THIS EXPERIENCE is something only found *within*, however, appears to be forgotten even by some seekers after light who long have comprehended that the Spirit's living substance cannot be attained by thought.

Many thus are eager to witness merely some sensational events in outer life, but fail to bear in mind that even the most awesome wonder they might physically observe can never grant their inner life the true illumination that lifts the darkness from all understanding, as here the knowing self becomes united with the Spirit's light itself.

Ultimately, even the experiences that one may have *within* possess their lasting value only as they herald the attainment of this oneness with the Spirit.

The highest goal to be achieved, however, is a form of inner apprehending that is no longer limited to one particular event.

What at this point will be experienced is the conscious sense of a NEW LIFE.

By means alone of this new *way of being* will all experience then become transformed, both in the realm within, and in the world without.

RESURRECTION

Now HAS THE seeking self begun to enter a new life.

A life of such abundant content that any craving after miracles and wonders, which earlier may have beguiled the mind, is then forever stilled.

What significance, indeed, might any "miracle" encountered in the outer world—such as the legions of the blind in every age would love to see—still hold for those who henceforth will experience the most ineffable of wonders *in themselves?*

The latter know that everything which even the most uncontrolled imagination might conceive of "miracles" occurring in the sphere of physical existence—assuming they could actually take place—would nonetheless remain confined to merely this material world, and therefore be completely worthless, void of all effectiveness, the moment when this earth's material body is abandoned.

THEY, TOO, INDEED shall witness magic energy in action, which even in this earthly life can bring about, by forces from a higher plane, what no material sorcery is able to effect; yet even this activity, which merely is concealed to *physical* perception, will not becloud their judgment; given that they apprehend, within the Spirit's light, that everything which in this manner may occur does no more than *expand* the range of physical existence, but cannot ever manifest the radiance of the living Spirit, whose power, far removed from all the like effects, reveals itself exclusively within the human being—and in that being's *spiritual self*—as in its own, eternal, one-begotten issue.

KNOWING THIS, THEY shall be helping those whom the eternal Spirit has prepared to serve as its embodiment in human form, and thereby seek to offer light to all who in this life are searching for the Spirit's light.

Far removed from thirsting after "wonders," they clearly will with open eyes discern the real miracles in daily life's events; and by the power of the light illuminating their own being they shall dispel the darkness that surrounds them.

They live the new, awakened life, whose truth the thralls of physical perception all around them may disdain, but cannot reach themselves as long as they remain benighted by their creature senses' darkness.

Those who are content to live entombed within the feeble glow enfolding them as mortal creatures of the earth, exist beyond the liberating help extended by the *Luminaries of eternal Light.*

None but souls resolved to *free themselves* shall here be granted liberation.

If they are earnest in their quest for light, however, they always ought to clearly bear in mind that "miracles" in earthly life are neither necessary, nor of the slightest use to serve that end.

The Spirit shall at all times choose the very simplest way whenever it would manifest itself in oneness with a human being's timeless self.

I harbor gravest reservations when someone tells me he feels called upon to serve the Spirit, but at the same time mentions certain "wondrous signs," supposed to verify the calling he received.

A heavy dose of vanity and intellectual arrogance is also part of the presumptuous demand that the eternal Spirit should reveal itself in outer life in special ways—by granting insights not accessible to all.

THOSE WHO TRULY are intended to encounter such experiences will face them unawares; and these events confront them suddenly, without their ever having sought, nor in the least expected them.

But then will an experience of this kind indeed be spiritually meaningful and lead one further on the path ahead.

To those who search for "miracles," however, only "hell" displays her skills; and all who would encounter a "magician" may rest assured a charlatan will fool them.

IF YOU WOULD find and enter that new life—the Spirit's life beyond the sting of death—then tame your fascination with mysterious things; but comprehend that God's eternal wonder is experienced only in your inmost self.

Admittedly, that innermost experience does not lend itself to boasting before others; but then I hope you will not blasphemously prize the Spirit's gifts according to their suitability to let you posture as a "chosen one" in public.

It well may seem incredible, but unfortunately I here speak from experience when I say that I have known of more than one who seriously believed his quest of unity with the primordial Spirit was, surely, in accord with spiritual law, yet who would at the same time miss no opportunity to brag about the "secret insights" granted him, in order to impress the uninformed.

In this way such a person merely shows how immeasurably far he strayed from the authentic path into the Spirit.

Be not misled by his ambition to display himself—a wretched mortal creature—in the spotlight of theatrical illumination; nor let him give you cause to be concerned, since you, an earnest seeker after union with the Spirit, have never witnessed wonders of that kind.

BEING ON THE path that leads to union with the living Spirit, you will receive your confirmation in a very different way.

In your external daily life there is no need that even the minutest thing must change.

Be cheerful with the happy, and sad with those who grieve.

"Enjoy the day" in such a manner that you need never shun responsibility to others for anything you do.

Firmly stand with both feet on the ground of this beloved earth, but do not first, by tolling every bell, announce that you are getting ready to raise your hands to heaven.

It is not necessary, nor is it even beneficial, that you are known by all as someone who pursues the path into the Spirit.

LET ME SAY that I myself was made to take this path and had to reach its end before I was allowed to enter the new and different ascent that was to lead me to my spiritual Brothers.

It has been many years since I arrived where very seldom in this mortal life a human being is admitted.

RESURRECTION

For years I now have publicly presented the teachings on the Spirit's light to all who understand my native tongue and way of writing.

Yet to this day there still are many who think they know me well in outer life, but are as unaware of what I do as of the work of any other person one respects and will accept because one sees him competently deal with life and its demands.

You as well should in the same way quietly pursue the path that you are meant to follow in your outer life; nor must you think it necessary to leave and to renounce the world if you would reach the Spirit's life within you.

That which you experience in your inner self is given to be yours alone.

Whatever you can give to others will bear its worth within, even if your own experience is not mentioned in a single word.

Do not speak of your experience unless you can be certain that doing so is absolutely necessary.

For all others, however, the things you do, or will reject, already offer lessons without words; and this example often will prove more effective than your efforts everywhere to talk about what stirs your heart and soul.

You still have far too much to cope with in yourself to even think of feeling qualified to give advice to others, unless they ask you for assistance.

A‌ll alone you patiently must make your way toward the eternal Spirit if you truly want to reach your goal.

Only by yourself can you discover the reality of your new life.

With yourself alone in your new life, you one day shall be able also to bring help to others who, like yourself, are longing to discover their own new life within.

CHAPTER TEN

FESTIVE JOY

Here the topic will not be the rousing festivals one celebrates in outer life, nor the revelry of those who only know that kind of happiness.

The festive joy I have in mind is one that thrives exclusively in solitude, admitting of no witness other than the celebrant.

Far too much I see you searching after outer feasts; indeed, I fear you may already have forgotten how to prepare a festival to celebrate with your own soul.

But even as the prudent rulers of all ages understood that human beings let themselves most easily be governed when the sour burdens of their daily toils on holidays are sweetened by high-spirited festivities, so should you likewise know about yourself that you most readily shall master everything that in you must be subject to your will if you are able not merely to control by force whatever may oppose you, but also to prepare a feast for everything that willingly obeys you, as soon as it shows signs of growing weary.

Such festive joy is far more needed by the soul than many of the best imagine.

"Man does not live by bread alone, but by each word that comes from the mouth of God."

The nourishing word of God, however, will not enter you until your soul is festively prepared for its reception.

During the time you are a "workshop" in external life—and that is what you need to be in everyday existence—you will have to be satisfied with any food the everyday may grant your soul; and while you are at work in outer life such nourishment will be sufficient.

From time to time, however, your soul may show itself fatigued; of this you will become aware when it no longer can receive the food provided by the everyday.

FESTIVE JOY

At such a time your soul craves other nourishment, such as the everyday could never offer it, however rich in inner sustenance that outer life might be.

These are the hours when you need to know you would do well to let your soul enjoy a feast.

You are not capable of celebrating feasts, however, as long as you remain a "workshop of the everyday," from which one never can entirely remove all dust and scraps of daily work.

You thus should know that you possess the magic gift within you to *transform* yourself.

It is your duty, to be sure, to function as a workshop in your everyday; but you are likewise granted festive hours to enjoy, when you are free to choose the form your soul's profoundest longing seeks.

In such festive hours can you transform yourself into a vaulted dome and celebrate the mysteries within your being.

You can make the sound of tolling bells and organ's thunder fill your soul.

RESURRECTION

Here you will yourself become the cantor of exalted psalms.

IF YOU DISCERN the meaning that these images would make you grasp through words, you long will have discovered the kind of *festive joy* your soul demands if it is not to wither in the drought of daily life.

You know the hours only too well when your soul grows weary and no longer will accept the nourishment sustaining it at other times.

At such moments, my advice is this: Do not then needlessly torment yourself but promptly let your soul enjoy a festive hour.

Retire to you room and close the door; or find a quiet place in nature where you will be alone and undisturbed.

Either choice will serve your purpose if there you can be by yourself. You even may be in the midst of people, so long as you are not compelled to speak.

ONCE YOU ARE completely by yourself, heed nothing any longer that reminds you of the everyday and of its toils and struggles.

You later will find ample time again to set aright and deal with everything that at the present would distract you.

Empty yourself of everything you feel devoid of festive joy.

Then, however, let your thoughts give form to the most beautiful, sublime, and perfect likeness of a human being your imagination can conceive.

Let that likeness come to life in you; and once it clearly stands before your soul—*identify* yourself with that envisioned image; and give no heed to any thought that seeks to show you how thoroughly—and not to your advantage—you still differ from this visualized ideal.

In your daily outer life you clearly do not yet resemble the inner image that you formed, which therefore dwells potentially within you; but no one can be certain that you will remain so faithful to yourself that one day you shall truly be its likeness.

Even so, for the duration of your present festive hour you should endeavor to forget what still are your shortcomings and defects.

RESURRECTION

In this, your present festive hour you are to see yourself in only the perfected image of a human being that you formed; and all things that conflict with its perfection you ought to disregard.

With this resolve create within yourself a consciousness of sacred inner joy and gratitude, without the least consideration of your usual practice of justifying first within your mind whatever actions you perform.

You have no need to worry and may trust me when I say that after your return into your daily life there will be many an hour left in which you can make up what in your festive hour you believe to have neglected in self-criticism.

It is of uttermost importance for your soul to be aware of all your human weaknesses and failings; however, it is even more important that from time to time you will allow your soul to see you in the form that one day you are able to attain, once you have become unchallenged master in yourself.

FESTIVE JOY

In hours of self-criticism you cannot judge yourself in too severe a light, nor deal too mercilessly with your flaws.

Yet do not be a fool and think that you could ever grow to be a "better" person by wallowing continuously in the image of defects that your self-criticism shows you.

Only those grow "better" who will act; those who recognize their failings and create, from their own selves, their individual ideal, which then they earnestly endeavor to resemble more and more.

The festive hours of your soul, however, are to loosen the inherent fetters that hold your thoughts and feelings bound, so that everything within you will be readied to conform to the ideal image you created.

Therefore I encourage you to let your soul enjoy such festive hours whenever it grows weary in the course of daily life.

From every festive hour of that kind you will go forth with an addition to your soul's dynamic energy that truly may astonish you.

RESURRECTION

You shall increasingly grow able to make your daily life obey your will, and even your most dismal hours will be lightened by your festive joy.

In the end, however, you thus shall come to know, already in your mortal life, that highest kind of festive joy that nothing here can any longer interrupt, because it is a constant testimony of *eternity*.

You will the sooner reach that lasting festive joy, the more consistently you let your soul gain strength in festive hours of the kind I here describe.

You should regard each day as incomplete on which you found no time for such a festive hour.

Do not believe your daily work and duties could prevent you.

Even though you may be toiling like a galley slave, you still can seize your festive hour, if you truly will; nor need it be an "hour" by the clock.

Renewed with unexpected strength you then may once again return to do the work your daily life demands.

CHAPTER ELEVEN

THE VIRTUE OF LAUGHTER

If you have never had the strength to free yourself from gloomy and depressing hours by your laughter, you truly do not know the precious gift that laughter is.

Perhaps you even feel disdain for all whose liberating heartfelt laughter lends them wings to soar above the obstacles that block their way.

You find it difficult to understand that some are capable of taming even the most searing pain by their ability to laugh.

Superficial and insensitive may seem to you all those who still can laugh when all around them there is only hopeless gloom.

RESURRECTION

Take care, my friend, lest you pass judgment on yourself by finding fault with those who have the strength to laugh!

To be sure, the proverb says that by his laughter one can tell a fool; however, it is no less true that laughter also will reveal the sage.

BY YOUR LAUGHTER you can release from oppression not merely yourself, but likewise all others around you.

How often has not heartily compelling laughter warded off some grievous harm!

Anger and explosive temper soon find themselves ridiculous when at the proper moment such laughter breaks the ice.

Despite this there are people who almost seem afraid to laugh and who will go to any length to show a strangely grim and sour mien when they see others laughing.

Some believe their dignity might be diminished if they were to laugh in cheerful company; others harshly discipline themselves, determined to surmount the follies of the world, and they dismiss all cheerfulness as folly.

And thus they show their foolishness where they regard themselves as wise.

MARK THIS, MY friend, if you are striving after harmony within your soul and seek to be united with the Spirit in yourself: I cannot take your efforts seriously until I know that you can laugh!

Needless to say, your laughter should not make you seem a fool; but on the other hand you ought not to avoid occasions to be cheerful.

And what is more: I find your spiritual striving suspect as long as you believe you must as far as possible forgo the gift of laughter.

I want to see you as a person who will never lose his sense of humor.

You still should have the strength to laugh where others long since would have seen their courage flee.

In your laughter I would like to hear your being certain that you truly shall attain the goal toward which you strive.

Your laughter is to tell me that you feel secure and have surmounted fear.

RESURRECTION

A RUINOUS DELUSION fosters the belief in all too many, even in this day, that they cannot approach the realm of God, or anything divine, unless they beat their breasts in woeful lamentations and bewail their "sinfulness."

You, by contrast, are to learn to mock your sin with laughter; for only if you recognize that foolishness alone had made you sin will you be able henceforth to avoid it.

You should become an object of self-ridicule when you recall the gloomy days in which you still were capable of sinning and thought you might find "happiness" committing sins.

IN TRUTH, NO feeling of remorse shall wrest you more effectively from sin than shall your liberating laughter at your foolish deeds.

And had you been immersed in sin up to your neck, you then should more than ever ridicule your former foolishness and learn to laugh at what you were.

For all the loud bemoaning of your faults, you never will undo what has been done.

Perhaps remorse may like barbed wire fencing enclose for you the realm of sin; it nonetheless remains for you as merely a "forbidden land"; and if you are quite honest with yourself you well may in your heart of hearts discover a feeling of regret that this now fenced-in land shall henceforth mark the limit of your freedom.

Not until you learn to laugh at your addictedness to sin will you indeed be able to escape it.

Only that shall truly free you from your appetite for sin.

No MATTER WHAT may lie behind you on the journey of your life on earth, it must not serve you as a reason from now on to avoid occasions to be cheerful.

If in the past you looked on cheerfulness as being the equivalent of "sin," you now should learn to recognize that radiant serenity can never have the slightest element in common with the folly one calls "sin."

You had merely been a victim of deception if you were able for a short time to succumb to the illusion that you could find enduring joyousness in "sin."

RESURRECTION

Laughing at your own beguiling blindness will guard you most effectively from ever trusting that mirage again.

The more you learn to laugh, the freer will your life become.

And as you learn to laugh more freely, you will more earnestly approach the things that let themselves be found by only serious endeavor.

Thus will your ability to laugh become a helpful gift upon the way that leads you to yourself.

With your laughter shall you then be able to confront and hold your ground against all danger.

And so you shall be liberated, by virtue of your laughter, from all the heaviness of earthly life that seeks to weigh you down.

CHAPTER TWELVE

SELF-CONQUEST

THE UNRESTRICTED SELF-EXPRESSION of their personalities has come to be a principal demand of modern human beings.

Nearly everyone believes to be entitled to such a life of unbound self-expression; indeed, I have met not a few who felt that living in that manner was their duty.

In sharpest contrast to these views appears the strict requirement that has in every age been stressed by all who sought to free their fellow mortals from the yoke of earthly bondage, and thus to lead them to the joy of self-experience in the Spirit's world.

Their requirement, however, was that all who meant to reach that goal had first to learn to conquer their own being; and this is summed up in what seems a paradoxical monition:

Only those who conquer their own being can truly find themselves.

APPARENTLY, THERE IS no bridge across the gulf between these two positions; and yet, the impulse toward desired self-expression, against the thirst for higher knowledge, remain opposed forever only if interpretation of the concepts will create that gulf.

So long as the desire to live life to the fullest confines itself to merely physical existence, it is clearly incompatible with the requirement to conquer one's own being, demanded by the Spirit.

Nor can the need to conquer one's own being be fulfilled if it is falsely understood to mean one has to "mortify" oneself in the denial of one's self-experience.

Ultimately, the demand to conquer one's own being is no more than an insight gathered by all those who were not satisfied with self-expression merely in the physical dimension, but who, instead, desired fully to express themselves as well in the domain wherein they felt to be the final cause of their existence.

The impulse toward the fullest self-expression is not in any way denied as such.

It is, instead, fulfilled far more completely; and thus the insight is attained that the most perfect form of self-expression can only be experienced after one has conquered whatever had obstructed the impulse fully to express oneself.

T<small>HOSE WHO ASSUME</small> that every possibility of self-experience can be exhausted in their merely physical existence, are thus consistent, according to their error, when they seek their fullest self-expression only in the physical domain, because they do not know that their desire for the fullest self-experience points to regions far beyond this mortal life.

Objectively to understand that longing, and to be able to guide it to its highest aim, one must have gained a clear conception of what the "human being" actually comprises as a spiritual reality.

RESURRECTION

One here must not be satisfied with taking only things into account that may be physically examined.

Considered purely as a product of the earth, the human being truly is no more than an abnormal animal, with all the qualities possessed by other animals.

Indeed, I even hesitate to look upon the human mortal as a "higher" animal.

And this applies not merely to a person's body, but also to the "psyche," a component human beings share with other creatures.

Yet this particular animal—in contrast to all other creatures—became the manifesting agent for a spiritual potency, so that in the course of thousands of years the psyche of that animal was likewise heightened and expanded, as a result of spiritual influence.

Nonetheless, that being's animal nature remained as such; and even were it to exist forever in its specific personal form, it never could in all eternity become transformed into the Spirit's substance.

Nor, for that matter, could the spiritual potency, which seeks to manifest its essence through this animal, in all eternity descend into the animal's condition.

On the other hand, this spiritual potency remains connected to an organism—an invisible body of the subtlest kind—which, although not either "extra"-, nor "super"-cosmic, can truly be considered "super"-physical, given that its substance, while it permeates the earth, does not in any way form part of the component elements that constitute this planet.

We here are dealing with the *cosmic, spiritual* human being in the form it functions closest to the earth; owing to its influence alone the earthly creature, in which it manifests itself, becomes transformed into this planet's *human* being.

Now the cosmic-spiritual human, in its form most closely bound to earth, remains inseparably connected with its manifesting agent, the mortal human creature, while the latter's life endures on earth; however, for the spiritual human being this connectedness may just as much become a cause for joy, as of the most tormenting agonies of hell, because the spirit's impulse to express itself may be not only furthered by the earth-born mortal creature, but equally resisted, if not indeed destroyed.

According to their norm, human mortals only sense their creature bodies' consciousness, which may be more or less affected by their spiritual nature's influence.

And that is true alike of learned and unlettered minds, of young and old, of potentates and beggars.

However, it is possible to break the fetters of that norm, so that mortal humans then are able to be conscious not merely of their creature state—no matter how uniquely differentiated it might be—but at the same time share the light-pervaded consciousness imparted by the spiritual nature of their being.

That goal can only be achieved, however, after the demand has been fulfilled of which initiates throughout the ages have spoken as the *conquest of one's self*.

SELF-CONQUEST

But this term must not be falsely understood; and those who long to rise above their consciousness as merely mortal creatures ought not to think they are required henceforth to renounce all elements of creature life; because the spiritual human self is needful of the mortal creature's senses if it is to manifest itself on earth.

To "mortify" and kill the creature's nature is a crime; no matter whether the intent to strangle only manages to paralyze its drives, or brings about the creature's death.

The ascetic who torments his creature body because it disobeys his will should not regard himself in any way superior to an individual committing suicide, who destroys his mortal organism in an instant; for the ascetic's action merely is less radical, but not in any way less reprehensible.

The only thing necessity requires is the restraint of all the creature's drives that one intuitively feels to be obstructing the human spirit's will to manifest itself.

Requirement is that the mortal creature's consciousness will recognize itself as such and thus desire to transcend itself.

RESURRECTION

That, truly, is the meaning of *self-conquest* correctly understood.

Its practice may bring forth the integration of the mortal creature's consciousness with the enduring self-awareness of the human spirit, and thus create a homogeneous unity both here on earth and for eternity.

Then, however, "death" has truly lost his "sting"; for clearly conscious of its unified identity, the newborn, spiritually integrated human being will leave this present life and find itself alive within the radiant substance of the Spirit's realm.

In its mortal body has the human creature thus achieved its own *redemption*, while at the same time setting free the spiritual human self, releasing it from torments of obstruction by the creature, which henceforth serves the human spirit willingly on earth, and through its earthly soul remains inseparably united with that spirit for all time.

However, if this integration is not accomplished in this present life, then it may be aeons before the "soul," whose elements survive the earthly creature, will be able one day to unite its consciousness with that of an eternal human self, and thus attain its own immortal, individuated life.

IN EVERY AGE there have been human beings on this earth who, already in their mortal lives, had unified the "creature's" form with "God," which is to say, had unified the mortal creature's consciousness with that of their eternal spiritual individuations; and all authentic spiritual knowledge that still survives on earth, however mingled with additions of minds without authority, is rooted in the insights of those few; for never has the Godhead spoken to humanity on earth but through the voice of human beings.

But everything revealed by those who had authority to teach, received from the domain of conscious human life within the Spirit, because they had awakened in that realm, has always been of help to only those who could be moved with concentrated will to strive for *self-conquest* as it is here described.

NO HUMAN BEING can "redeem" another; but one who knows the way on which "redemption" is achieved can show that way to others.

RESURRECTION

To make them willing to pursue that way, he neither has the power, nor the right.

And, truly, human mortals are reluctant to confront the fact that in their present state their consciousness comprises no more than the senses of the earthly creature.

Reluctant in particular are the self-righteous minds who long have found, as they believe, "salvation" in one religious system or another; reluctant likewise are the learned intellects that see themselves as "rich in spirit" because their keen intelligence is able to dissolve whatever they encounter.

I certainly could understand if minds impeded by their own convictions rather will dismiss my words with scorn than put their substance to the test.

Frozen solid, like ruts on muddy roads in winter, remain the mental tracks in countless human brains.

According to eternal law, however, no one shall be able any longer to undo his fate when finally the day has come that he must leave this earth.

SELF-CONQUEST

Today, this very moment while you read these words, the time has come for you to take account of where you stand.

Today you still are able to decide yourself, and your decisions manifest your will.

But your considering the things I have to tell you will be worthless as long as you are not resolved with all your energy to act according to their guidance.

In any case you would be wise to disregard your preconceived ideas; for you shall not be able to form objective judgments until the day when finally *self-conquest* has liberated also you from the oppression by the earthly creature's life, and you have come to know the consciousness of your eternal spiritual self.

Your task is not to conquer me and what I say, but to discern and overcome the error which is rooted in yourself.

CONCLUSION

All eternal wisdom rests in *being*;
It cannot be discovered by mere thought.
Only by Reality of Being
Is truly lucid thinking's power wrought.
Thinking that is merely mental labor
Is bound to lead the searching soul astray.
Timeless Being grants to thoughts its favor,
Whose radiant grace sheds light on thinking's way.
From Life itself all timeless wisdom flows,
Mere thinking never wisdom's light bestows.

REMINDER

"Yet here I must point out again that if one would derive the fullest benefit from studying the books I wrote to show the way into the Spirit, one has to read them in the original; even if this should require learning German.

"Translations can at best provide assistance in helping readers gradually perceive, even through the spirit of a different language, what I convey with the resources of my mother tongue."

> From "Answers to Everyone" (1933), *Gleanings*. Bern: Kobersche Verlagsbuchhandlung, 1990